IP

Pisgah Press was established in 2011 to publish and promote works of quality offering original ideas and insight into the human condition and the world around us.

Copyright © 2023 Mamie Hilliard

Published by Pisgah Press, LLC
PO Box 9663, Asheville, NC 28815
www.pisgahpress.com

Cover photo by Henry Collins Hilliard III

Author photo by Susan Culler

"Live Your Poem" Raven art by Damaris Pierce

"The Call: Mamie Hilliard," courtesy Shelley Frome

Jacket design by Damaris Pierce

Photo collection courtesy of the author

All rights reserved. No part of this publication may be reproduced, stored in a retrieval system, or transmitted, in any form or by any means, electronic, mechanical, photocopying, recording, or otherwise, without the prior written permission of Pisgah Press, except in the case of quotations in critical articles or reviews.

This is a work of fiction. All the characters and events portrayed in this book are either products of the author's imagination or are used fictitiously.

Library of Congress Cataloging-in-Publication Data
Hilliard, Mamie Davis.
Something New About Something Old/Mamie Davis Hilliard
Library of Congress Control Number: 2023912079

ISBN: 979-88-502-5257-1
First Edition
August 2023
Printed in the United States of America

Something New about Something Old

Poems and Musings
by
Mamie Davis Hilliard

Pisgah Press IP
Asheville, NC

Acrylic on canvas by Damaris Pierce 2021

Dedication

To Linda Irene Todd, now singing with the angels

Acknowledgments

Poetry is a big part of how I make sense of the world. It allows me to look more closely and feel myself into my own experience. I desire to share these poems, to reflect how my life journey has been affected, and inspire others.

While I am happy to write in solitude, I have arrived at this point with the influence and assistance of generous people. I am forever grateful.

The inspiration from teachers, seasoned poets and fellow students has illuminated my path. This is also true for so many people I meet and observe, who help me see that there is poetry in everyone's life.

Thanks to Andy Reed at ArsPoetica for your keen eye and professional expertise.

Susan Culler, I am grateful for your support and attention to detail, and I respect you.

My children, grandchildren and great-grandchildren, I can see the future in you, and you give me hope. I am forever thankful for your presence in my life. To both of my grandmothers, thank you for encouraging me to work on reclaiming my soul through writing.

This collection of poems came from a large body of poetry that was birthed over the past few years. My good friend, Damaris Pierce, took on the task of editor and project manager and was instrumental in bringing this book into existence. This journey collaboration brought us a sincere friendship and I am grateful for her patience, momentum and expert language skills. Damaris holds up a mirror again and again so I find my way home to myself. The laughs and hugs have been icing on the cake!

Mamie Davis Hilliard

Table Of Contents

Acknowledgements xi
High Tide 1
In the Wings.. 2
Chosen and Chalk Dust 4
Is Mother's Coat a Good Fit? 5
Wars and Rumors of Wars 6
Modern Tyrant 7
The Best Gift 8
Woman in the Tent 9
Ladies of the Night 10
The Thing in the Way 11
Visiting Grandmother.. 12
The Garden beside the Church 14
Sunrise – Sunset – My Log Cabin Home........................ 15
Where Is the Purple?... 16
Grandmother, How Shall I Carry Your Name? 17
I See You.. 18
Haiku Collection 20
Longing to Create 21
Who Am I? Who Are You?... 22
The Third Daughter 24
Worth the Burn 26
The Captain "Shows Us the Ropes" 27
A Great Miracle 28
Reason to Get Out of Bed 29
Mountain Morning 30
I Ask Gabriel 31
From My Cabin Porch.. 32
A Blessing for Silviafest 34
Show Your Colors 35
A Sudden Winter Storm 36

A Journey: From Words to Images	37
The Cost	44
Shoes to Fill	45
February in Florida	48
A Natural Gift	50
Haiku Collection 2	52
Becoming	53
Pentecost on the Mountainside	54
Sit a Spell	56
Anatomy of an Argument with Someone You Love	58
The Log Room	60
Ponder These Things	61
Meet the Trickster	62
I Can Not Do That	64
Butterfly Effect	66
A Lament on the Tragic Death of a Young Friend	67
The Mellow Tick-Tock of Time	68
Daniel's Path	70
I Salute You	72
Looking for Home	74
My Hiding Place	76
A Place for Believing	78
I Am Too Tame	79
Haiku Collection 3	80
Star Light on Your Skin	81
The Story of the Seven Tunnels	82
Enough for Now	84
By Some Mad Grace	85
Nothing Left to Do but Dance	86
The Call: Mamie Hilliard, by Shelley Frome	89

Something New about Something Old

High Tide

The moon, waxing
Calls to the wave
Who, dips and rolls
Not tonight, on my way out

Moon cycles, dauntless
Calls again
Wave, demure, responds
Ripples high, moon smiles

Cool moonlight
With a drop of indifference
Very romantic, you say
Show me, show me, right away

Moon cycles every month
I am woman
Feel my tug
Cycle with me

Tonight, you are the moon
I am the wave
You become full, round, bright
I roll, crest and foam

Meet me on the beach
We will wax and wane
Come together high tide
Good night moon, good night wave

In the Wings

I wonder, I often wonder
Who wrote the script
For the drama of being human

Each night falling into sleep
Theater of Passing Time invariably haunting
Dreams come revealing time without measure

Here in slumber
A blessed mini-death
A rehearsal for the starring role

Knowing this, how to prepare?
Where is the script?
Who can tutor?

My heritage believes in God
Creator, Lover of creation
Giver of free will: develops our own character

Life reveals a prompter for those with ears to hear
The trickster, archetype of surprise
Prefixed by wonder, foolish and clever

Nature's life cycle holds surprise
Birth, death, new life
Does a wise fool honor surprise?

Somewhere between birth and death
Mystery touches
Wonder looms

Something New About Something Old

Listed, on the playbill, big performance
"Total Surrender"
Today's role, tomorrow's surprise!

Wearing a body at curtain call
We will no longer need costuming
Spirit will wander through the crowd

Mind cannot fathom the after-party
Stop! No need to solve this
Love life, affirm mystery

Each must play their starring role
No tryouts, no casting call-back
Being born gives the part

Here, take my hand, trust
At the Still Point, peace
Hold me until my cue

Chosen and Chalk Dust

Never chosen first
By our classmates
We know he stumbles
Over his own shoe strings

Elbert Clay Newton
Why are you
In my dream this morning?
A fourth-grade memory

Miss Woodall, teacher we all love
Chooses you to clean
The blackboard erasers
Big smile comes on your face

Along the blackboard, you gather them all
Hold them tight in your arms
They spurt out and fall
Get dust all over your shirt

Teacher sees and says
"You may choose a friend to help"
Big tears form, about to spill
You look at me, I know that feeling well

Out in the school breezeway
Me and you
Have fun cleaning erasers
Banging them together

Chase each other In the yard
Two friends laugh til it hurts
Chalk dust everywhere
And we don't care

Is Mother's Coat a Good Fit?

Timing releases the Trickster to appear
And appear again for the next generation
How big would your surprise be
To hear what your grown child can see
She learned from you?
Now watch the Trickster spin
To the other foot!
Your mother, hearing your
Revelation of what you learned from her

My daughter moved back
Across the country
Is California full of people
Trying to escape?
My head tells me not to grieve
She's doing what I taught her
Experience life fully
Craft your own identity
What about things I taught her?
It would surprise me to the point of denial

Call to mind things when questioned
It is revealed to you
You learned from your mother
Things she would deny but you know
You know
Who your authority was
Remember the things now
She taught you
Your own mother taught you!

Wars and Rumors of Wars

Their eyes grow large and round
They stare at me, my young friends
Yes, I remember the day
Pearl Harbor was attacked

Seven years old and building
A play house under the dining table
Hush, Mama says in a strange, harsh voice
I want to hear this news

We sit together in Dad's big chair.
The news was garbled noise to me
We sat in silence while she listened
My Uncle Jimpsey was on a ship docked in Pearl Harbor

My eyes grow large and round
When I hear my own Grandpa's story
He, not yet a man, must act quickly
His widowed mama shouts to him

Run, Raeford, run, hide the hams in the smoke house
The Yankee soldiers headed our way
They will take every bit of meat we have
Quick, think, we don't have a lot of time

My heart aches as I imagine the heat in 1942
Mama, why are we leaving in the middle of the night?
Where are we going? Can Daddy come too?
Surprise and confusion: they were ordered to the internment
  camps

Tyrant

Hello, I am Donald J Trump
Self-crowned
Emperor of these United States
My role: divide and conquer

My tactic is zero-tolerance
Of any idea, law or person
That is not of my linage
I am King

Give me no more of your tired, poor
Huddled masses yearning to be free
Not in my Kingdom!
Only beautiful mothers with orange-haired children

The Best Gift

Christmas morning
Joy to the world
In my stocking
Motel Six

Mary had a baby last night
A star shining bright
Like a light in the window
The Christ is born again

Believing is not a gift
Wrapped and under the tree
Believing is planting
Gathering around the manger
Needing a savior
Hearing yourself say
I believe
Remembering your mother say
We will go as a family
To church this day
Believing is devotion
One day to the next
One generation to the next

Woman in the Tent

Then, there is this woman
Homeless, the chit-chatterers say
I don't, at all, see it that way
Her home is her tent
Taut-tied to tall trees

She wears mystery
She tailors to fit
Is she a single mom camping out for a bit?
Is she goddess Daphne, fleeing a god
Or simply nature's daughter, sizing her fit?

Waves of moonlight bounce on her tent
Fiddle music floats in the air
Wood Nymphs peep out in the dark
She offers her picnic table by chance
All talking at once, they begin to dance

First light, back into the woods they go
Handmade treats they leave on her table
Without words, their life stories show
Simply made of sticks, stones, and string
With my own eyes, these I have seen

The winds come, blow and blow
Her tent, tight-tied, still stands
Weathering storms, her own demands
Morning light she comes out to pray
No one to stop her or demand what she ought say

My dog and I walk close by her tent
She peeps out, joins us, now hell-bent
We walk and we talk until spent
She is Mystery
And her home is her tent

Ladies of the Night

Early dusk
Still light enough to see
Up the hill
Past the church
Into the woods
On the hunt
For Lady Slippers

They share their beauty there
Careful, a misstep
Will crush them beyond repair
Look to your left
A group of nine

Dressed alike to our delight
Leaves of bright green circle
Puffs of pink

Dirt brown anklets
Cuff each slender stalk

The Thing in the Way

Dear Young Man
Your grandmother hears you
Child of my child, now nearly grown
Want to buy a handgun of your own
Not for my permission you ask
Only recognition of your attention to task

Dear Young Man
Your grandmother sees you
Child of my child, now handsome and true
Your life story told in tattoo
Souvenirs, look-like-treasures, are many
Your journey, bound for adulthood
Cost you plenty

Visiting Grandmother

Each night she and I kneel beside her bed
She in her long muslin nightgown and cap
Me in my plaid pajamas, pigtails and sunburned face
She taught me to pray
So natural for her to engage Jesus in a trusting way

Jesus, tender shepherd
hear me, bless thy little lamb
tonight in the darkness
be thou near me
keep me safe til morning light
all this day thy hand hath led me
and I thank thee for thy care

I felt afraid, a little afraid of this presence
Grandmother invited into our room
Something very genial, all around us
Never could make out a form

Big 200-year-old house
Avenue-wide hall down the middle
Ceilings so high
A child's prayer could be granted
Before it left the room
We played in upstairs rooms
Knew for sure they were haunted
Ghosts of family members came often

Unrestricted access to
"The Plunder Room," my favorite
Tangible memories of daily life, piled together
Children long ago, ten boys and two girls
Four sons fought two world wars
Three blue stars, one gold star

On a Veteran-issued white silk flag
Proudly hung many years in the front parlor window
Now hangs honorably in
Not-to-be-thrown-away section
Gold star son buried at sea from the Ticonderoga
Grandmother's faith never wavered
Her mother-grief expressed in poetry

My Laddie's Grave
"My laddie sleeps in the deep blue sea…"

Grandmother was a story teller
Each held a moral
The wee shy flower, not easily seen
Named by Jesus "forget-me-not"
Lame man carried by the blind man
Each helping the other

She encouraged us to see and touch life
Search for ways to be of use
These vivid revealing memories are dusty
Heavy with time
Now grown sacred

Summertime visits with seldom-seen cousins
Makes us friends, no matter how little we have in common
Other than our fathers being brothers
We climbed Mimosa trees by day
Played Backgammon til bed time

The Garden beside the Church

Before the dream
This little plot of land lay fallow
Seeds blew in and chose to stay
Mother Nature says, "let 'em play"

Rain spatters last year's dry leaves
Sunlight calls forth the green
The loving spirit lets them be
Free

One day we choose
Yes, this will be our garden
Tall weeds dance, English sparrows sing
Each living thing brings its own gift-ring

We who are friends with mystery
Come now to this garden to find ourselves
We come with hope to meet other selves
Past and present who gather here

Welcome, come in, sit a while
Look around you, feel the energy
Enjoy the gifts from nature as they appear
Be aware of their beauty while they are here

Sunrise – Sunset: My Log Cabin Home

Folding back the patchwork quilt
Out of bed before sunup!
This woman I never knew
The long-awaited day is here

She and her family are moving
Into their first home
Dovetail, chestnut log square
Dog trot down the middle there

She needs no alarm clock
And checks the blanket
Long awaited day is here
Many years of Army housing are history

"The rock fireplace draws real good!"
Soon she builds a fire, boils some coffee
No time yet to sit by the window
Watch clouds over the Craggies

Where Is the Purple?

You can make phone calls
Day and night
You can debate the different sides
You can march
You can protest

People who live peacefully
With pride in their community
Get honest pay
For honest work
With enough to eat for self
And family
Will not be manipulated
By fast talk

What is the answer?
It's not red or blue
Where is the purple?

Know that
Who you are
I also am

Grandmother, How Shall I Carry Your Name?

On the daybed in the corner of your big dining room
Like manna from heaven, my baby bottle full of treat
My very first memory, drinking milk, warm and sweet

Grandmother, I am child of your child
The family tree branches and branches
Now I, also am a great-grandmother

Your hand reaches toward mine, I stretch to follow you
A blessing falls and fills me, warm and sweet like fresh milk
"Story Teller," a heritage I receive from you

Childhood visits to your white antebellum home
Memory maps my way, I love this place
The sweet smell of purple lilacs along your path

The rhythmic creak of your rocking chair
Backgammon game board open and ready to play
Recollections make me smile
This is you, Grandmother

Every night beside your bed we kneel and pray
You in a long white muslin gown, matching cap
I in plaid pajamas, blonde pigtails, sunburned face

You engage Jesus like an old friend
Your words, out loud, on bent knees, cradle me
Your friend will also be my friend, Grandmother

I See You

Outside my window
On the hillside, Trees
Yesterday you were not there

Today I see you
Immediately
I am yours
You are mine

Leaves spiral around me
Flying
Floating
Falling

I sit hypnotized by your ability
Simply to let go
How do you do that?

Bare branches rub
Against bare branches
They push back

How do you know
When to do that?
When to turn the other branch?

Each Tree stands right where it belongs
Belonging brings its own peace
Recognition, its own contentment
I nod to the trees

Something New About Something Old

You play 'Simon Says' in the wind
You dance when you feel the spirit
Yet, you are strong and anchored
I like you

I feel the spirit
And dance in the wind
Where I belong is where I am
You like me

Dedicated to Susan Culler

Haiku Collection 1

renter trashed the house
benign neglect left hard feelings
new tenants bring love

                              they come to visit often
                              fill the house with laughter
                              good friends leave soon after

she smiles when sailing
tho' rarely wins when racing
simply loves to sail

                              wish I had done that
                              then it didn't come to mind
                              now it will not leave!

morning light comes in
walks across the ceiling
seems it missed the bus

                              we want to renovate
                              can not pitch our memories
                              we put them all back

Longing to Create

Being original is not easy
A tease, a whisper, a gasp
I give myself completely to the task

Mystery
Father's mystery
I want to create

Sound distracts
I close my eyes
Surprising hush hovers

The Source embraces my longing
Unravels my
Tangled threads

She asks "What are you thankful for?"
Beau, loyal dog asleep at my feet
The inlet's cleansing dance
My steady heartbeat

My longing finds words
"Why this loyalty to my longing?"
Created in the image of God
A lesson from childhood

Five senses give me no clue
It is in my longing
My soul comes through

Who Am I? Who Are You?

Today my view is all awry
Today as from a box
I look — so many angles
No place to take a stand!

A moral quandary
I do behold, a reality
Foreign to my senses!
Is there a right? Is there a wrong?

Friends of friends
These Drag Queens are
Blatantly and cosmetically
Appearing as other!

The bearded faces
Wear lipstick and mascara
Tight red dresses
Over-padded breasts

Rhinestones all a-sparkle
Six-inch platform heels
Long dark curls
Falsetto "B-I-N-G-O"

All dressed up
A place to go. A job to do.
Am I seeing Burlesque? Theater? Clowns?
I hear only nervous laughter!

Where is the entertainment
To drive away the blues
To give diversion
To the weary watchers?

Something New About Something Old

Drag Queen Bingo, the Gay Bar
My impulse, to sanctify!
For whom? The gathered crowd?
The Queens? Myself?

A glance shows it amusing
To those around me
Like dancing bears or
Seals on rolling wheels

Another look at the Queens
Is it degrading?
Cheap? Juvenile? Trashy?
Am I so different from them?

Am I some former Presbyterian
Needing to distance myself
From smothering Calvin doctrine?
Am I too rigid to see humor?

Am I able to appreciate
Their attention and pride
Choosing a special dress
Time spent on make-up

What disguise am I living?
Does subtle or secret make it better?
Is less conspicuous marketable?
Who am I? Who are you?

The Third Daughter

Daddy wraps me in wood-stove-warmed blanket
Puts me to bed in a cold bedroom
Three years old and I love my Daddy

Fourth birthday gift, Sugar, a brown and white Shetland pony
First ride I fall off, catch my foot in the stirrup
Sugar drags me to the barn, tears my new birthday pants and
    my hiney

Older sister Beth lets me go to town with her, goes to meet her
    boyfriend
I wait alone, she gives me her pocket knife to hold
I know she will come back for me

Uncle Robert loses his job, comes to live with us
We sit on the porch every night to smoke his pipe, we just sit
Sometimes we talk about our garden or riding in Daddy's pickup

Middle sister Marty gives me a Toni home perm
Birdie, our collie dog, starts having puppies; we go to watch
My hair gets frizzy all over my head

Mama washes supper dishes, I dry and put away
We play "I Spy" and have fun together
Mama doesn't play very much

Learn to count, four more than three
Older sisters teach me three with one over it
More than four with one over it; Marty draws a pie

Fridays, Mr. Moon, in old pick-up stops by selling fish
Teases me "hear my name? I light up the moon every night"
I do know this is not true, don't know what to do with his teasing

Something New About Something Old

Drag Queen Bingo, the Gay Bar
My impulse, to sanctify!
For whom? The gathered crowd?
The Queens? Myself?

A glance shows it amusing
To those around me
Like dancing bears or
Seals on rolling wheels

Another look at the Queens
Is it degrading?
Cheap? Juvenile? Trashy?
Am I so different from them?

Am I some former Presbyterian
Needing to distance myself
From smothering Calvin doctrine?
Am I too rigid to see humor?

Am I able to appreciate
Their attention and pride
Choosing a special dress
Time spent on make-up

What disguise am I living?
Does subtle or secret make it better?
Is less conspicuous marketable?
Who am I? Who are you?

The Third Daughter

Daddy wraps me in wood-stove-warmed blanket
Puts me to bed in a cold bedroom
Three years old and I love my Daddy

Fourth birthday gift, Sugar, a brown and white Shetland pony
First ride I fall off, catch my foot in the stirrup
Sugar drags me to the barn, tears my new birthday pants and
  my hiney

Older sister Beth lets me go to town with her, goes to meet her
  boyfriend
I wait alone, she gives me her pocket knife to hold
I know she will come back for me

Uncle Robert loses his job, comes to live with us
We sit on the porch every night to smoke his pipe, we just sit
Sometimes we talk about our garden or riding in Daddy's pickup

Middle sister Marty gives me a Toni home perm
Birdie, our collie dog, starts having puppies; we go to watch
My hair gets frizzy all over my head

Mama washes supper dishes, I dry and put away
We play "I Spy" and have fun together
Mama doesn't play very much

Learn to count, four more than three
Older sisters teach me three with one over it
More than four with one over it; Marty draws a pie

Fridays, Mr. Moon, in old pick-up stops by selling fish
Teases me "hear my name? I light up the moon every night"
I do know this is not true, don't know what to do with his teasing

Something New About Something Old

I steal cigarette papers from Mr. Blinson's country store
Wanting to roll rabbit tobacco from the pasture
He catches me, never tells my parents. I really like Mr. Blinson

Mrs. Barbee teaches piano in the Methodist parsonage
She never gets new furniture
Church members give her their old when they get new

My first-grade boyfriend Joe and I get mad at his mama
She makes him write with his right hand
He tells me writing is easy with his left hand

Joe and I play doctor in the crawl-space under his house
We take turns being the doctor
I am not telling my mama what we do

We adopt my brother Ray at six months old, I'm five
Mama promises I can give him his first bottle
Aunt Eloise comes and takes over, holds and feeds him

"Mamie will be jealous" I hear the adults say
"She has always been the baby"
My mama was not teasing me, I know I am still her baby

Worth the Burn

I dipped my morning toast
Into the cup of
Scalding cocoa
It dribbled down the side
A childhood memory
Puddled on the table

Just as mama said
The scalding
Will lose its ache
But the lesson it will take
Some chocolates
Are worth the burn

The Captain "Shows Us the Ropes"
Balance – Boundaries – Beauty

She assigns seats, seeking balance
Then noses the bow toward the big river

The boat planes, the wind rises
I hold my hat...relax...enjoy

Pass several inlets, "no...not yet,"Captain says
Suddenly, starboard we go into Soldiers Creek

The outboard-motor-noise dashes across the water
Drowns out nature's well-mannered woods-hum

Our speedy passing seesaws each floating dock
Rocks a group of men at work

From my childhood, my father's voice I hear
"If you are not going to work, don't disturb those who are"

We stare at them, wait for them to wave
No, not going to happen

Nature's raw beauty is rank and file
A well-kept yard, clean boat, their style

We joy-ride, slice the water, leaving a wake
So bitchy it bobbles boats berthed on both banks

Amid the motor noise and the mythic wake
The Captain stares straight ahead

Surprising us, she U-turns the boat
I ask her, "what happened?"

With great feeling, she responds
"I had a beautiful epiphany"

A Great Miracle

Every time I let my mind wander
I try to explain myself to myself
Thinking I can do that I get confused

Am I living someone else's life?
I want to go home

Michael Bublé, Canadian singer
Sings my feelings
He makes it sound like his feelings too

I am ten years old
Every week on the radio
I hear the Lone Ranger
He is my hero

Grandmother Davis holds me
Tells me stories and listens to mine
Life is easy to understand
She is my hero

I am the Grandmother now
And I listen to my own life
I hold myself and tell myself stories
Like my Grandmother did

I can see through negative moods
Even laugh at them
I see them as absurd dramas and illusions

I am able to move freely from
Dark emotions that rule my life
That is the greatest miracle of all

I am home

Reason to Get Out of Bed

Bidden or unbidden
God is present
Not that it happens
But that it happens to me

I see birds, free
Being birds
I want to be free
Being me

I want to see
The far-wild-blue
I want to smolder
With the campfire, warm and true

Look, someone
Moves my way
We catch sight of each other
I want to stay

I want to go
A dire risk to linger here by the fire
And sit close
Feel warmth, find words

This is top bid
A reason
Every morning
To get out of bed

Mountain Morning

Night air tickles my nose
Cold ground seeps through my breeches
I stand to welcome the crowning sun
Dawn is birthing day. I knew it would!
Assisted by a star caught on a mountain top

Wing sleep from the east ridge
Sun's rays take a big breath and sneak up on the cove
A new day's along the way
Rising, the sun steps over the dark
Clutter from last night

Trustworthy mountains sleep where we left them
Rushing streams sing and dance
Joyful praise to the light
Tree limbs stretch and
Scratch both sides of the sky

Snuggling clouds awake to nature's hum
Rising to care for their young
Mothers of every ilk feel the same urge
Morning prayers from the wind flutter the leaves
Yellow school bus stops then goes down highway nine

Green leaves prepare for fall
Ready for change to cycle in
Hovering clouds play tag with the mountains
Giving hope they will move out like the tide
Exposing sand bars of resiliency

I Ask Gabriel

Yesterday
I killed a redbird
Once a beautiful crested cardinal
His light feathered body
No match for my speeding car
I am sad

Wherever you are tonight
I ask of you, Gabriel
Blow your horn tenderly
And receive
His tiny winged spirit
Unto you

From My Cabin Porch

I rise early
Paddle to the porch
Cool mountain air
Tickles my nose

Sun's first rays
Reflect a brilliance
On my neighbor's window
Announces the miracle
Like a newborn's first breath
The moment speaks in tongues

In the distance
The mountain ridge line
I want to be the mountain ridge
It views both sides
Remains grounded
Strong

Today the sun rises
Rises on same-sex legal unions
Love, honor, equality
I raise
My near-empty coffee cup
Cheers!

From the south
I feel a gentle breeze
Gives me a pleasurable quiver
The backyard ferns
Kneel and rise
I say my mantra and meditate

Something New About Something Old

Chipmunks scurry in and out
On the rock wall
The red fox waits
For the right moment
Mother bear calls her cubs
Let's pilfer the neighbor's garbage

Beside the path
Under a sourwood tree
Our beloved Beau-man
We buried him last week
The dog who tried so hard to
Be who we asked
His nature told him to herd
Now he is free

Time for the yellow school bus
Kids call it the Yee-Haw Wagon
It tops the mountain
Road circles, then a quick drop
Like a carnival ride
They all holler "Yeeee-Haw"
The bus stops at our drive
My daughter boards and waves
They head down highway nine

A Blessing for Silviafest

In the beginning
There was only cold and dark
On the first morn
The sun crowned in the east
Hope comes to this valley
Blessed be the light

Mother Nature hiked the John's River
On the third day
There arose from her satchel
Budding trees and flowering shrubs
Mountain peaks and rushing waters
Anticipation comes to this valley
Blessed be the beauty

Time brought two men towing a rainbow
With a dream in their heart
And sweat on their brow
Together they birthed this campground
Fulfillment comes to this valley
Blessed be the circle of campfires

A mountain breeze
Whistles in the valley
Bullfrogs and hoot owls harmonize
Two women hear the melody
"Music, a feast, a fest!" they exclaim
A family reunion comes to this valley
Blessed be Silviafest!

Show Your Colors

Leaves whirl
Flying, floating
Riding the wind

I see you standing in awe
Watching
Grandson, Grandson

This you also can do
Who knew?
Your Mama knew, your Daddy too

Let it be, let it be

Connection all your life
Not much at all of any strife
You were bud, sprout, leaf

All the while limb
Held you tight
Who will let go first

Limb or leaf?
Grandson, listen
Listen to the wind

Your turn, your turn, your turn

You are stout-stemmed
But your reckoning is beckoning
Let it be, let it be

Show your colors
Let the seasons write your journal
I was here, I was here, I was here

A Sudden Winter Storm

Then all of a sudden while reveling in my OK-ness
In the dark of the night
I wonder about natural things
That live outside in all kinds of weather

I see the pine trees sway
Their shallow roots clinch the ground
A mother bird knows to cover her newly hatched babies
In nature's architect-designed nests
Ants are rushing home single-file
Racing the last falling rain drops and loud kazoo sounds

Mother Bear feels the storm coming
She gently nudges her new cub to move on
They saunter back to their winter-rumpled den
A yearling cub looks on from his pose in a tree
Longs for mother's comfort

Are the wild turkeys smart?
They clump in a knot and face into the wind
Trusting their feathers to shed the storm

I see a flying squirrel glide
Gutter to my neighbor's garden
Living up to their name
Now an endangered species
Will they come back?
I hope so

Many of the nests and dens outside our cabin
Are made cozy with brushings
From our fourteen-year-old Corgi dog
She sheds profusely
We leave fluffy mounds
Free for the taking

A Journey: From Words to Images

Eight months old

Mamie Martin Davis 3 years, 1937

Mamie with her cousin and first pony Sugar

Age 13, 7th grade

Mamie and Hank Jr Hilliard right before his departure to Vietnam, July 1967

Walter and Christine Davis, parents

Ordination, 1993

Grandmother Hannah Davis, poet, mother of eleven children, here at age 99

With grandchildren Maggie and Abby, feeding the birds

Mamie with life-long friend, Louise Mitchell Clark, on the left with Louise's daughter and grandson

Mamie and life partner Susan Culler, 2014

Mamie's children Christine, Hank and Lynne, 2006

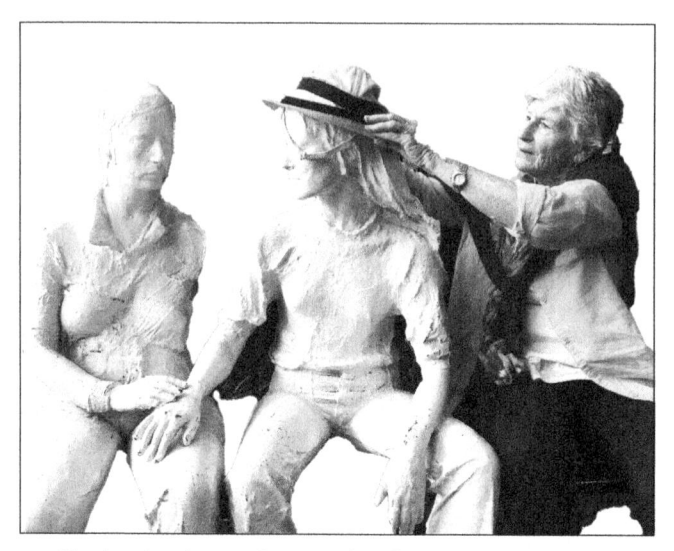

Sharing her hat in Greenwich Village, New York, 2017

Susan and Mamie at North Myrtle Beach, 2019

Mamie, Lucy and Damaris Pierce, editor,
at work, 2023

Sculpture "Sister Rising," created by Damaris Pierce in honor of Mamie's two sisters and all her unknown sisters

The Cost

From across the big pond
Word just arrived, a suicide bomber

Boy-jihadist
Killed my neighbor's young soldier son

Both boys
Believers in their mission

Both mothers
Hug their country's flag

Both mothers
Set their son's place at the table

Both mothers
Look for baby pictures

I grieve with both mothers

Shoes to Fill

Who is knocking
At my back door?
Give me a minute
I'm coming!

There he stood
Just like the young man
I saw as a child
In the tintype on grandmother's dresser

Likeness so great it startled me
Intense blue eyes
Looking at me from
A strong young face

Come in
I don't know your name
But I know you
Not even thinking

He'd find me a bit crazy
You are my grandfather!
I am Ruthie's boy, he said
With little boy pride

Brought these sweet potatoes to you
I'm not a little boy anymore
I am a farmer now

What's your name, young man?
It ought to be Raeford!
You look so much like him
Your profile, your stance

Do you carry his name?
What do you know about
The man who was
Your great-grandfather?

My name is Jamie
I am an organic farmer
Hope you like sweet potatoes
Mama said I should come visit you

I do like sweet potatoes
Thank you, Jamie
I like that you came to see me
A peaceful pause passed between us

Want to know why I'm really here?
This man, this family legend
Everybody talks to me about him
Was he really that great?

Can you imagine
How hard it is
When genes give you
Big well-worn shows to fill?

Something New About Something Old

I wish I could
Plant a crop
Of shoes that fit me
I know how to grow things!

Jamie, you are already preparing the soil
Be diligent, be daring
Your yield will be worth your work
Your harvest will be familiar

I have been shopping
For shoes all my life
I was born wearing my mother's
Tightly laced vintage "Dr. Locks"

Standing there inside my back door
I looked down
At my bare feet
We both smiled

February in Florida

Ripples on the river inlet
It rushes out to the gulf
Wind rises
Mullets jump
Tilapia strut their taste
Hiding from the hook
One more cast
You can cook

February in Florida
Valentine's in the air
Remember love's sway
Celebrate our first meeting
That hot Fourth of July day
The fireworks

You walked up beside me
Your friends, my friends
Introduce us to see
If love at first sight
Might be
It was good eight years later
Over and over
Yes, ever new

Something New About Something Old

Love at first sight
Oneness I feel
Yes, nine years
It is real
Nothing separates us
Ordinary things
A first time feel
Surprise of first sight
Freshness gives

Each moment lives
Each daybreak
First sight
All over again
Thank you
Giving and receiving
In Love making
Abandoning all else

A Natural Gift

By the sea
By the sea
God's presence surely must be
By the sea

What makes you sure?
I walk the sandy shore
Outright vastness all around
A special feeling comes over me

I walk barefoot in the sand
A natural gift
To feel what you feel
To enter what is real

A storm blows through
Broken Shells lie on the beach
Hodgepodge of bits and pieces
Lying there, waiting

I wait with them
We sit together on the shore
My nagging need
Be a perfectionist

Surprise, surprise
Mother Mary reveals in the sand
A natural shell
Manifest by the sea

Something New About Something Old

Or was it the storm, or me?
Broken and beautiful
The message I hear
God's presence is near

This shell I want, said my friend
If you dare to share
A keepsake offered by the sea
Our walk, you and me
Honor a faith, found in my youth
God's promised presence is truth

Haiku Collection 2

walking uphill fast
makes headlight, heart heavy
going down I just waddle

> night is very dark
> all stars have gone to bed
> don't forget my wish

it gets dark early now
sun and earth are doing it
what is their relationship?

> trees whisper to each other
> have you turned yet? no, have you?
> have you a fall plan?

gentle hand gloves hers
she works with Grandpa's hatchet
legacy to his favorite

> golden retriever: the dog
> golden years: the geriatric time
> fetch only what's yours

Becoming

Seeking life's meaning
A summons to pilgrimage
Comes to me

Quickly packed and prancing
No time to wonder who is driving
I get my ticket, jump on board

Surprise, surprise
Bidden or unbidden
The Trickster drives the bus

Seeking life's meaning
I am stock still for a moment
Linger with those I love

In time's enormous waiting room
Abandon clock's mythology
Tick-tock, tick-tock

Just be

Pentecost on the Mountainside

> *All gathered in one place*
> *A sound from heaven*
> *Like a strong wind*
> *The holy spirit comes upon them*
> *"I will not leave you comfortless."*
>
> Acts 2:2...John 14:18

Take highway nine south
Pass a generous grove
Each tree animated
Now leaning in
Feeling the spirit
Now drawing back

Gaining a consensus
They sway together
Stage left, several oaks
Holding their leaves
Move to a Calypso beat
Music by an unseen band

Then comes a foxy wind
A bossy bitch
Move with me
When I come by

Oaks and elms
Sourwood and locust
Move in concert

Pentecost on the mountainside
Each hearing in their own tongue
Each moving to their own understanding

No tree left out
Whenever the spirit-wind passes through
I will not leave you comfortless

This morning
The trees are motionless
No wind
No dance
Steadfast in knowing

Sit a Spell

On your 88th birthday card
Two chairs by a door, face the yard
One sister to the other
Girls of the same mother

Sit with me, where once we stood
Together in our childhood
Shared moments in short pants
Traditional values, our family's dance

I, the younger, more freedom was allowed
You, older, always the first furrow plowed
Sisters now in our eighth decade
Still marching in life's parade

Middle sister always caught both ways
Compassion, memory of her, stays
Early, I knew my older sisters were different
Learning which one to go to, was significant

A hug from Martha was a "shoo-in"
A "how to" from Beth when I had "no clue in"
In the large two-story home built of gray stone
Close-knit family, I never "went it alone"

Two sisters, one brother, two Collie dogs and a cat
Wild animals, farm animals, we had all that.
Salesmen, strangers and the corset lady
Remember we teased Mama, now we don't, we're eighty!

Something New About Something Old

All those people, the front door used
Knock, no answer, knock again, confused
All who knew us well, back door
All who came to sit a spell, back door

Those who did not know where to park
Those who made our collies bark, front door
Now, you and I live three hours apart
Fortunate to have someone to drive our cart

I have no more words to rhyme
So we will just have to mime, our thoughts
I know you don't like me to send poems like these
Read this one, written just for you, please

For Big Sister, Beth
Love, Mamie

Anatomy of an Argument with Someone You Love

Today you hold the mirror
Facing me with your accusations!
They hurt me to my core!

Same mirror however
Casts a shadow on you
Reflection comes both ways

What is happening here?
Our future together presses me to ask
Will you join me to take on this task?

Do you see only my actions?
Will you also consider
your contributions?

Am I only able to hear the mirror holder speaking?
Dare I risk a look at myself?
Tension shatters the mirror

Shards fly
Piercing words travel back and forth
Now, two bleeding hearts

Finally egos rest, commitment shows
Love asks to make the first move
Gradually kind words flow

Question becomes
Which way toward reconciliation?
Wisdom responds:

Go!
Dip three times in cleansing waters
Of the River Jordan

Forgiveness rides a carousel
Next time 'round ask love to hop on
Recognize anew the importance of her presence

The Log Room

It is every visitor's choice
Why is that?

Because this room
Is womb-like

How can that be?
Right angles, square, hard

It is an enigma
Close, warm and cozy

Most of all
There is spirit in this room

One more question
Is it a spirit or the spirit?

Answer that for yourself
I invite you to come

Go!
Dip three times in cleansing waters
Of the River Jordan

Forgiveness rides a carousel
Next time 'round ask love to hop on
Recognize anew the importance of her presence

The Log Room

It is every visitor's choice
Why is that?

Because this room
Is womb-like

How can that be?
Right angles, square, hard

It is an enigma
Close, warm and cozy

Most of all
There is spirit in this room

One more question
Is it a spirit or the spirit?

Answer that for yourself
I invite you to come

Ponder These Things

The hawk swoops down
Without a sound
Snatches the baby squirrel

Breakfast, Christmas morning
Screeching
First the baby, then the mother

Stunned into silence, what did I just see
Mother squirrel quickly
Scurries down the tree

My child saw it happen
She quivered like a drum
Take it all back, she begged

I looked around for help
To grapple with nature's way
What to do? What to say?
Is there a plan I don't understand?

My child and I stand arm in arm
In the warm sunlight
We don't talk about this terrible fright

I will invite Mother Nature for tea
Mother to Mother
We will be

Meet the Trickster

Round and round
Seasons hurry
Horns sound
Count down
Ball drops
Celebrate
Start over

Turning point
The still point
Makes the dance
Looking back
Best choice
Poet's voice

The big ring around
Types abound
Patterns gather
All the same
Yet not quite
Meet the Trickster!

Short shy
Simper smile
Sexy salutation
His role to play
Hero and clown
Giver and receiver
Hiding wisdom

Many names
Equalizer games
Foolish and clever
Agent of enlightenment
Now needs new words
Too many times
Been to the well

My voice, your hearing
Whose turn to bring
The meaning?
Say a word of prayer
Make a prayer
Write a prayer
Hide a prayer

I Can Not Do That

I can not stop watching her
Does she know?
I try not to stare
Her face is oh so rare

Near-late for church
Does she cope by being late
No trace of self-pity in her gait

Two pews ahead and to my right
I squint my eyes real tight
Too far to chat
Wish we could do just that

Her face, her first hello
In the mirror every day
I wonder, does she
Sing or pray

Someone spilled the puzzle box
All the king's horses
All the king's men
Can not put her face back together again

I take another look
Ugly, comes to mind
Because it is all she can find
I try to figure, was that so bad?

My mother's voice I hear,
An ugly duckling stage, my dear
You will grow out of it, no fear

Something New About Something Old

She holds the hymn book and
Sings by herself
Is there someone special in her life?
Help her carry this apparent strife?

We all stand, hold hands, sing the closing
Does the man beside her take her hand?
I look away, tears come, definitely not in my plan
Let there be peace on earth, let it begin with me

Why did she come to church?
Could it be to find someone
Hold her hand, love her?
Make her feel like a beautiful swan?

I can do that
But I will have to love her
From a place already taken
I can not do that

Butterfly Effect

Little bird with agile wits
You come with your flock into my midst
Happy you do not scare away
Tell me, would you like to play?

Incidents from my life's journey
Fall like seeds in the grass
You peck and scratch
Outwit the others

Do you seek Easter eggs
Hidden in tall-grass-myths?
The bright colors draw me close
A red egg in green clover excites me most

Do you run with the wolves
Find meaning reading myths?
You show me where your interest is
Then you hide the key

A Lament on the Tragic Death of a Young Friend

Camping in south Florida
The sad news comes
A young friend was killed
Her beloved brother was driving
This morning I walk the dogs
On the levy dividing
Our campground from the Everglades
As far as I can see
Marsh grass ocean
Blowing waves in the wind
Flock of big black birds
Lands on the grass

Lord, have mercy on us
The weight of our grief is too much
Can we withstand this heavy darkness?
Open our eyes to see answers
Revealed in nature
When the heavy black bird
Comes and perches on
The slender blades of marsh grass
They bob and bend with the weight
But they do not break
Have mercy on us and give us faith
We, too, would be resilient
Like the bending marsh grass

The Mellow Tick-Tock of Time

We call it the Star Clock
In December it will be 144 years old
You can still see the small gold star on the glass panel front
The 16-inch-tall rosewood cabinet aged beautifully
Turn one key, winds the movement of the hands
Turn the other key, winds the striker
Both keys have six generations of finger prints

Counted time for Mamie and HC, fifteen homes
Henry C. Hilliard, Jr., wife Mamie Martin Davis Hilliard
Children Lynne, Hank 3rd, Christine
The clock came into the Davis family in December 1871
One hundred years before my baby child, Christine, was born
With five dollars, my great grandfather bought the Star Clock
A Christmas gift for his wife, on his return from the Civil War
Mother to daughter
To Hannah Barham Davis, my grandmother
Grandmother lived ninety-nine years counting time with the Star Clock
Mother talks to son
Hannah Martin Barham Davis to Walter Armstead Davis
Grandmother Davis, Hannah, gave the clock to my father, Walter
One of her 11 children, 9 boys and 2 girls
As a child, I heard it ticking when the big house grew still and quiet
It sat on the mantel in the dining room

Something New About Something Old

Father talks to daughter
Walter Armstead Davis to Mamie Martin Davis
My Daddy gave me his mother's clock
I cherish it and give it to my son
When all is quiet now I still love the soft tick-tick
The passing of time is sweeter when the Star Clock is counting
Mother talks to her son
Mamie Martin Davis Hilliard to Henry Collins Hilliard, 3rd
In my eightieth year I, Mamie, give the Star Clock to my son, Henry 3rd
Now the clock counts time for him and his family

One day
The mellow tick-tock of
The Star Clock
Will count time
In the home of
The seventh generation
May it be

Daniel's Path

I saw him at a wedding
This old woman watched
Her granddaughter get married

I was all alone
In a foreign country of beliefs
Feeling I was an outsider

Daniel showed up by my side
He too one of a kind
Studs in his lip and disks in his lobes

His tattooed hand on my elbow
Escorted me with great care
People could see our happiness

Later, I hear, he left his place of work
To help his younger brother
Go to a new job

Because he, too, had been
Down a similar path
Daniel knew the twists and turns

He wanted to help
Already contributing
In more ways than he could know

Still learning, being patient with himself
His hardest job
His best lesson to share

Something New About Something Old

Learning about people
Nuances of intimacy
Whom to trust

Living each day
With as much courage
As he can muster

"You will choose wisely many times"
"You will miss the mark sometimes"

"Who am I?" becomes "I am a child of God"
I belong — I am loved
Because I am

Some days don't question
Just be
Other days glance at the mystery

Dare to look for yourself
Then wait
Be open to answers disguised

Stay close with nature and
With those who love you
I am one of those

Your grandmother,
MaMamie

I Salute You

She is small in stature
Low in rank

221st Army Hospital
Heidelberg, Germany

No one doubts her when she drapes
Never-used stethoscope around her neck

She is a general!
Who is Private Jones?

Staff responds just short of saluting
Her command: the maternity ward

"New mamas love her"

Scrawled above the doorway as if
More for entertainment than information

"Maternity Ward"

High windows throw light
On only two walls

Of this large irregular shaped room
Giving it an unexpected degree of warmth

Single metal beds
Bulge from interior walls

Something New About Something Old

Vibrating and chattering like steel drums
When occupied

Army blankets cover rigid white sheets
Severe pillows yodel unwelcome sounds

What is it about this room?

"New mamas love it"

Jesus Christ Superstar
Who do you think
You really are?
Year's big Broadway musical

Private Jones allows full volume
From the boom box by the bed

She nixes dancing between
Nursings so we learn new words

To all songs and
Struggle with meaning:

Sunday school material or
Blasphemy?

"New mamas love it"

Looking for Home

An old chestnut log cabin
Grounded and mountain surrounded
Gifted my parents to me
My forever home to be

A motor home rolling
On paved blue ribbons flowing
A new love, a new start
An open home for my heart

Old Testament teaches old truth
Ten commandments
Brought down from the mountain
Look to the past, the fountainhead

New Testament, a new way
No need to grovel, we all have feet of clay
Mother, no apple, no original stain
No need for cleansing in river's rain

There is an angel standing
One foot on the land
One foot on the sea
Body and soul in balance, free

Southern lawyer, Atticus in his home town
His grown daughter returns
Many changes found
A town, a Dad she does not know

She cannot stay, she cannot go
No longer Scout
Not the home town she came to see
All this made incarnate by Harper Lee

When a child, think as a child
When an adult, put away childish thoughts
Unexamined shoulds and oughts
The journey ... is home

My Hiding Place

I am nine years old
School starts today
Fourth grade is scary
Up early, dark outside

My hair won't do right
Mama fixes oatmeal, not hungry
I have a cool, new backpack

My teacher last year liked me
Mama said my new teacher will like me
I don't like her, she is mean
All my friends are taller than me

Back home
The front door squeaks
My house feels spooky
The back hall is so dark

Climb my apple tree in the back yard
Tell it my secret
I came home before the bell rang
No one can see me cry

Mama left chocolate cookies
On the kitchen table
I can climb, eat cookies, at the same time
Mama calls me a monkey

Something New About Something Old

Leaves are gone off my apple tree
I can see the cows over in the pasture
The babies are black like their mamas
I watch them nurse

The robin's nest in the maple tree is empty
I saw two baby birds fly away yesterday
Mama bird came back, looking for them
I just know she was

A Place for Believing

Maybe
Just maybe
Fairy tales are true

You and I are of this world
We share its bittersweet mystery
But we are also from somewhere else

We are from Oz, Narnia and Middle Earth.
We were not born yesterday
But are like children, looking for our hearth.

No matter how neglected or forgotten
There is a child in each of us
A place for believing

This Garden was created for believing
Maybe fairy tales are true after all
Pause and peruse, how dear the spirit here

Who among us can say
When or how it will be
When something easters up

To remind us of a time
Before we were born
Or after we die?

We greet the spirit of our memories
Let the luxury of nature's beauty
Speak silent supplications

Come again and again to this Garden
If your basket is empty, fill it
Again and again with what you find here

I Am Too Tame

To write poetry
Afraid of the feral in me
Fear will not let me open the door
It is over there, across the sea
I have no raft

Excuses, excuses!
Remember the first time with her
First touch on fire
With desire.
Where are those words?

Go to the wild side
Wild west
Wild animal
Wild card
Just when I think I am ready
I am too tame

Haiku Collection 3

rain on a dirt road
children playing in the mud
5 cents for a pie

                                  first time 'round wind sound
                                  cyclone destroys a whole town
                                      forgiveness circles next

cool nights
sun sets early
firewood

                                                  shoveling
                                               more snow
                                        more shoveling

door to door
outstretched hand
orange candy

                                    crisp juicy apples
                                    picking on a ladder
                                  lunchroom box and straw

Star Light on Your Skin

Evening pulls down her shades
Darkness falls, now come charades
Each star begins to twinkle
Playing with the night

Near our campfire
Dancing shadows leave no clue
Inlet waters ebb and flow
Which way will she go?

Over there a snoozing 'gator
On that slanted log
Is there danger in the dark
Or in the sleeping croc?

Is excitement
In the mojo of the campfire or
The passion in her warmth?
Each a likely suspect

yes, danger could be there
Show your feeling
If you care
Do it, if you dare

Thinking, good for thinkers
But feeling, really feeling
Star light on your skin
This a treasure
Beyond measure
Dear, dear friend

The Story of the Seven Tunnels

Going up the mountain, dawn is tugging
At the dark
Southern Railway train is chugging
The familiar sound is hugging
Memory I know by heart

Tingling with excitement
Cousin Betty and I catch the Choo-Choo train
We are on our way
Summer camp for a whole month stay

Coal burning engine a-churnin'
Wheels a-turnin'
Sit by an open window all day yearnin'
Can't get there soon enough
Marked with ashes and soot
No matter to us

Two happy little girls
Circle up Old Fort Mountain
Round and round and round
We pass through seven deep dark sleeves

The train enters
The train leaves
Light, dark, light, dark
Seven times
Recorded history brings dark to light

Convicts, mostly black-skin men
Blast these mountains
Lay these rails
Forced to tunnel through
"Get 'er done, what you gotta do"

A parsimonious politician
Brags to fellow law makers
Work the prisoners
They are takers
You can make them money-makers

Too hard the heart
Too steep the grade
One hundred thirty-nine black men
Buried far from home
In a shallow grave

The peak price
These prisoners paid
For the railroad legacy
They have made

Hear us
Hear us
Their souls cry back
The train chugs on down the track
Clickety-clack, clickety-clack, clickety-clack

Enough for Now

I meditate
Spend time
Tucking the raw edges of Life
Around the moment

It makes a trampoline of sorts
I gather up the scattered pieces
Once, twice, three times
I bounce

I catch a glimpse
Of "The View"
It is enough
For now

By Some Mad Grace

It's holiness they hunger for
By some mad grace
A morsel is mine to give

I give as best I can
To those who cross my path
And they, searching
Tell me their stories
Pause, stare into space
Take my hand, back away

They look for mislaid words
To voice their longing
Tell me I am not alone
That I know I matter

And so, whatever
Of Christ
Of comfort
Of companionship
I have found
On my fitful, fruitful journey
In the Lull of stillness
With kid gloves
I open
My satchel of sacred souvenirs
Surprises from the Trickster
Inklings of God
And I offer them

Nothing Left to Do But Dance

You died
Your oldest granddaughter called
I can no longer hit 'favorites' on my phone
Hear your voice
Many phones I have had
Your same number
Like your steadfastness
I know by heart
Fifty-five years, friends
Nothing left to do but dance

Social Worker brought your children
Stork brought mine.
We celebrated each arrival
Our daughters
Imitated our friendship
Yours passed first
Mine grieved with you

We took turns being host
For our friendship
We acted always as friends
Only now do I see the
Beauty in that trust
I miss you
Nothing left to do but dance

Something New About Something Old

I wish you were here
We would celebrate your leaving
Our last good bye
You were already hearing
Voices from the other side
"Go on," I urged
"I am right behind you
I will bring the wine"
Nothing left to do but dance

Dedicated to Marigold Arnold Chesson

Mamie Davis Hilliard

The Call: Mamie Hilliard
by Shelly Frome

Nestled deep in the southern reaches of Black Mountain, with the Blue Ridge Parkway hovering in the far distance, Mamie Hilliard finds herself sheltered by her beloved log cabin and embraced by the peace of the natural world.

In the near distance, she can look out on the sourwoods beginning to bloom "with their little white things hanging down." She fondly notes they're the first ones that turn a bright red, the bees make the very best honey, and Black Mountain is known as the sourwood town.

And so, whether she's reminiscing, exploring her world or getting down to the business at hand, you instinctively know that you're in the presence of a memorable person, one whose rhythm blends in perfectly with each and every endeavor.

Looking back, she recalls coming from the farm in North Carolina to Camp Merri-Mac for girls on Montreat Road. At the time, she was well acquainted with animals and nature but hadn't been in touch with many people. Presently, she was quite taken with the mountains and her fellow campers and soon discovered her parents had come here during their courtship. In fact, her daddy had worked summers at Blue Ridge Assembly. Now that there is a boys' camp, her grandsons carry on the legacy. As a matter of course, legacy and continuity become two more telling touchstones:

"There are six of us who live here in Black Mountain from those camp days and are still in touch, including Annie Hall, who everyone knows."

But it's not as though she's always lived an easily evolving life. She married an army chaplain, went around the world with two children in tow and had a third child in Heidelberg, Germany. You could just simply say she's developed a highly centered approach over the years: a perspective that stood her in good stead when she decided to become a member of the clergy.

At the age of sixty, she was ordained at a Pentecostal seminary during the time that she and her husband moved to Chattanooga, Tennessee. It all came about as she envisioned a spiritual component to a Masters in Social Work. As a fifth-generation Disciple of Christ who came from a long line of clergy and educators, the Pentecostals gave words to her quest:

"Pentecostals feel things. It comes from the Pentecost when the spirit came and everybody spoke in their own tongue. That's what Jesus promised he would send to comfort us. 'I will not leave you comfortless. My spirit I leave with you.' That's what they say happened at Pentecost at the gathering during biblical times. It's the holy spirit that happens in your heart and mine."

It comes then as no surprise that she would find spirit in the cabin she inherited from her folks in 1985. It also comes as no surprise the one-hundred-and-six-year-old structure is made of hard chestnut that has lasted through many a season, and that spirit extends to the mountain people themselves:

"Living here is in my DNA. It's home because of the spirit that's here. This house was built by people who were mountain people. I say that because I love the mountain people. They're authentic, they're real. They don't have roles to play. You take up for each other. You don't talk about it. You just know you do. The logs in this cabin were cut by an old whipsaw cutting back and forth. I feel it in there. I feel the original folks and my parents when I'm in here because they all had the spirit. I feel a real heritage that's been loaned to me for a while and I will pass on to my children. I've lived a lot of places with my army husband but this is a special place."

In retirement, ministering only on occasion and on an individual basis, she's now writing poetry and calling it *The children of my old age*. She feels it comes from within herself. She births each and every verse. Struggles but tries not to struggle, to let it come to her. She once put aside a poem after two weeks, then sat by the fire and wrote it down in ten minutes. And it was good. It said what she wanted to say.

It goes without saying she finds something Pentecostal about the process. The spirit entering at a certain point and dwelling within. Some day she will bind each and every poem in a single volume.

All in good time.

This article was previously published in
The Black Mountain News, September 3, 2014.

About Pisgah Press

Pisgah Press was established in 2011 in Asheville, NC to publish works of quality offering original ideas and insight into the human condition and the world around us. Our releases include fiction, nonfiction, philosophy, history, memoir, children's literature, and other genres. The Pisgah Press imprint ArsPoetica was established in 2012 to help regional NC poets see their work in print.

To support the tradition of publishing for the pleasure of the reader and the benefit of the author, please encourage your friends and colleagues to visit www.PisgahPress.com or contact us at pisgahpress@gmail.com.

Poetry collections from ArsPoetica at Pisgah Press

Donna Lisle Birton
From Roots to Wings $14.95
Letting Go $14.95
Way Past Time for Reflecting $17.95

Jim Carillon
Centered $12.00
This Virgin Page $12.00

Mamie Davis Hilliard
And To See Takes Time $12.00

Jay Jacoby
Lessons Learned & Unlearned $14.95

Martin A. Keeley
Fragments $16.00
Shifting Tides: Stories & Poems $20.00

Peter Olevnik
Buried Pennies $14.95

Nelson Sartoris
Brain Slivers $12.00
On Wings of Words $12.00
Unsent Postcards $14.00
With These Hands $15.00

Nan Socolow
Invasive Procedures: Earthquakes, Calamities, & poems
   from the midst of life $17.95

The Poets of OLLI*
Barricaded Bards: Poems from the Pandemic $12.00

*Osher Lifelong Learning Center, UNC Asheville

For information:

Pisgah Press, LLC
PO Box 9663, Asheville, NC 28815
www.pisgahpress.com

Made in the USA
Middletown, DE
23 July 2023